# *Leavings*

by

Lenore Hirsch

Laughing Oak

Napa, California

*Leavings*

---

## ACKNOWLEDGEMENTS

The following poems have been previously published: "Hunter" and "Reprise" in *And the Beats Go On* by Redwood Writers, 2014; "Joints" and "Leavings" in *Third Wednesday*, Vol. IX, No. 1, Fall/winter, 2015-16; "Heart Geography" in *Literature Today*, 2016; "Night Chorus" in *First Press, Collected Works from Napa Valley Writers*, 2017; "Gates and Chimneys" and "Prayer for Dying" in *Phoenix: Out of Silence . . . and Then* by Redwood Writers, 2018.

I want to especially thank teachers Judyth Hill, Ana Manwaring, Gary Silva, and Iris Dunkle for their encouragement, and the many writers with whom I have participated in critique work: Marilyn Campbell, Barbara Toboni, Amber Starfire, Sarita Lopez, Marianne Lyon, Jim McDonald, Lynda Burris, Susan Imboden, Renate Halliday, Doug Brozell, Karen Stern, Betty Van Patten, Pam Jackson. And everyone who comes to open mics and cheers us all on!

# INTRODUCTION

There are many kinds of poetry and many reasons for writing it. I write a poem when I am moved by something I see, hear or feel and I want to express that emotion with as few words as possible. Thus, my poems are generally short and simple. I'm not interested in allusions to historical or mythical figures or places. Although I enjoy playing with words and love metaphors that add layers of meaning to all kinds of writing, my style is pretty direct.

This collection is divided into seven groupings: nature, places, politics, introspection, relationships, grief and loss, and word play. My fondest hope is that you, dear reader, will grasp and share the feelings I had when I wrote them.

# Leavings

## Writer's Therapy

You can't be wishy-washy if you want to write;
you have too many decisions to make:
this  word or that,
one paragraph or two,
long sentence or short,
fancy words or simple,
and the constant decisions come
not just from observation,
not just from skill,
not just from practice,
but from your writer's soul—
that somehow knows
what sounds best,
what says it best,
what words are yours.

I.

# Night Sky

vast black sky engulfs me
spills icicles of light
shimmering patterns of ox and archer
have moved since summer
dance in a new dark meadow
canopy more round and deep than the lake
I cannot see beyond
yet I have walked to the other side of the lake

if I could pierce the dark dome with my spear,
would the brightness bleed out?
or do powerful gods look down while I sleep
do they laugh at me with my hungry spear
do they control the bison on the plain, the wind, the rain?

## Patterns

butterfly wings
waving panes of yellow, red
trimmed with black

zebra stripes
onyx and ivory
fade afar to brown

live oak branches, twigs
lacy filigree on sapphire
hashtag sky

coral arms brown and grey
crisscross shadows shimmer
weaving fishes yellow blue

nature's patchworks
all the art I need

## Cycles

two tangerine butterflies
recently crawly things
now fluttering windowpanes
catch sun
swirl and float
to butterscotch blossoms
summer celebrants

a silent grey shape
on the awning
mourning dove
still, alone
flies buzzing

I struggle with stepstool
clothes brush
ladder, rake
to cruelly scrape
and scrape again
the silent weightless
thing
onto the ground
wrap it in plastic
put it in the trash

and sadly remember
a spring dove's nest
on the porch light
parents watching
twin babies

and two tangerine butterflies

## Looking Up

I.
looking up
looking for sky
my eyes follow
a forest of
glassy-eyed
concrete monoliths
up and up and up
steel grey chills
smoggy stench of industry
feeling lost, insignificant
nameless


II.
looking up
my eyes follow
brilliant green giants
gorgeous in their
asymmetry
bright and shadow
playing off the needles
piney scent
fills olfactory receptors
and soul

shorter aspens
tinkling silently
in the cool breeze
chirps and burbles
softly sliding brook
up and up and up
the pines lead me
to the topaz sky
and I see myself
as if from
the tiny airplane high above
insignificant
but not nameless
sister to the trees
part of the living all

## Night Chorus

I love the sound of the sea
waves pounding shore
constant crash and slide
tow me out of myself

but at night
awakening to the roar
I long for quiet
moments to live
in my head

far from the shore
the summer night
hosts an orchestra of
crickets
insects
frogs
a muffled jingle bell band
jee-jee, jee-jee, jee-jee

I prefer their rhythmic sounds
to silence
they sing of life
throbbing, humming, chirping life
of me, one murmur of many

the sea
for all its beauty
is dead
when we've killed the
fish
plankton
microbes
it will still pound the shore

I love the sea
but crickets more

## Everywhere, birds

blue jays squawk
robins strut on sun-baked fence
hummingbird seeks sweets,
zooms from blossom to blossom
doves nest on porch light
bluebirds feed chicks in their own wood house
crows keep guard on high
shout warnings from tree tops

all around
chirps and cheeps and beeps
fall from tree and bush
a symphony of avian chatter
reminder that despite
slamming doors
rumbling roads
grinding machines
barking broadcasters,
wilderness, lustrous and magical
remains
if only we will stop and listen

# Rescue

Earthworms glide across
glistening sidewalk
refugees from rain.

By afternoon
you may wriggle back
to the comfort of mud.
If you linger on
the sun-dried pavement
you'll be stuck.
Then I, savior
of innocents,
may pick you up
cast you back to
safety.

Like me, you guard
your tiny spark of life
struggle to breathe
eat, procreate
until sick or old
or squished
by God's strange magic
the light goes out.

## Blue Jay Way

As I open the back door
to let out the dog,
as he scurries around me
and onto the deck,
a flash of blue and black
across the sky
I stop—
not just one blue jay
two jays diving
and squawking,
two brown birds
hovering, swooping,
the hired security contingent.

The dog runs after
a blue fluffy thing
on the deck
and I realize
it's a fledgling,
can't fly.
I scoop up my predator,
ducking to avoid the
wings, the screech.

Baby jay scoots
behind a pot
as I approach,
wanting to know if he's injured,
beneath the bird wrenched sky
he flutters across the yard
takes cover under a bush
and moves every time I bend to see him.

I give up, take the dog inside, wait,
and later, check the yard—
no blue jays or brown birds
no fluffy baby
just a few tiny feathers
floating on the grass:
freedom's discards

## Bobcat

Late morning sun
strikes
tallgrass hillside
wild graveyard
only rocks and trees
mark the creases
where the departed lie

Buried in memories
I don't notice my dog
wandering away
across wildflowered grass
until I look full on
see him walking beeline
to a boulder perch
held by
sharp-earred cat
unmoving, watching

I whisper "wait" into the silence
suspend breath
he stops
turns
returns to me
alive

## Shape Shifter

Dawn, shifter of shapes,
silences the night,
silences midnight of worn edges,
drowning senses.

Dawn paints over crickets
blows out the lantern
in the children's tent
and summons them to table.

The house takes on a new day
we struggle to awaken
to voices calling, phones ringing
reminded to reenter life, blessed home
and all the joys we know.

II.

## Kitchen on Billerica Road

scarlet linoleum floor
slopes to back garden door
holds a table of yellow and chrome
matching chairs
faux tile on white walls
my family home

pighead cookie jar
on the counter
near breadbox of tin
under the window
springtime sun
blazing in

tea kettle sings
children shout outdoors
smell of cold, damp coal
from basement
fly buzzes at the window
behind billowing lace

golden corn fresh picked to boil
ripe red watermelon drips
down chins
homemade pizza, doughnuts, pies
childhood gathered round
the comfort table

place where we flocked
to cook, to eat
for parties, discussions
whatever our needs
I feel the grounding still
the sense that all was good

I cannot return
to that kitchen of my dreams
but memories will always
bring me back to
love, my safe place
the place where I belonged

## Patagonia

soft sheep
icy shore
towering silvery slopes
grazing guanaco
glacier roads
penguin-dotted isles
courting cormorants

pisco sours
bass and hake
meaty empanadas
beef, beef, and beef
dulce de leche everything
but especially ice cream
even in winter

sheep in the shearing shed
sheep on the barbee
lamb on the plate
wool so heavy
left unsheared kills the sheep
how can I eat
this sweet beast?

who am I here?
shutter snapper
peso spender
smiling greeter:
"buenos dias"
diner
judge
too cold in the wind
too warm in the cabin
too long on the plane
dinner too late
breakfast too early
bus ride too long

yet I am in Patagonia
and Patagonia is now in me

## "pueblo"

the word
reeks of conquistadors
priests
a foreign tongue
while to the Tiwa
it is simply
has always been
home

they speak of life
not on a timeline
but as eternal union with those
who came before
red willow ancestors
who hunted in the mountains
fished Blue Lake
carried water from the river
taught their young

today they leave the pueblo
venture out into the world
for education, training, travel
but they return
for ritual, family
play and work
to know again connection to the earth
the people
a living organism
always and forever

## South Africa

Jo'burg: housing crawls over
flat green landscape
sandy ridges stripped of gold
mansions on tree-lined hills
look down on mismatched
squares of brick, tin, earth, rubble
brick bungalows
tin-roofed squatter shacks
makeshift stalls sell
bananas and bandannas
broad ivory smiles in
gleaming ebony faces
cascade of languages
punctuated by Zulu clicks
a common history that aches
with mingled pride and pain

wide angle horizon
bare lacy trees
tall green grasses
hold grazing
impala
buffalo

elephants
giraffes sprouting from bush
birds in motion
lifting
flying
landing
insects harmonizing
buzzing
whistling
big cats' throaty exhalations
smells of grass and dung
all set against
a turquoise sky
filled with towering cloud animals
fading to pink and grey
layers of
serenity

## Hunter

Stalking prey,
hours pass,
waiting, looking, waiting,
hungry for reward.

Victim appears.
I choose, commit,
ready to shoot.
Eyes meet eyes
for a heartbeat.

Escape abandoned,
prey submits,
destiny fulfilled.
I am satisfied
until the next time.

Weeks later,
prey returns
in stunning photos.

## Safari Eyes

eyes scan savanna
jeep jumps in rutted track
bush, tree, termite mound

dark shadow on tree limb—leopard?
no, dead wood
brown smudge behind bush—antelope?
no, termite mound

scanning
hour after hour
animal shapes
burned into the retina of my imagination

long neck in shadow—giraffe?
no, dead tree

Wait!
jeep stops
breath stops
leaves rattle, darkness moves
alive—elephants!

## Bitterroot Mountains

snowy peaks summon my love
in sun fire reflections
like a baby's magnetic smile
boast their staying power—
a lover always ready for more
confident
rock solid
here forever
compared to me

the range lies down across my view
in deep sleep
a blanket of dreams
dreams of bravery, discovery
majestic thrones caress earth and sky
in my lifetime
scarcely moved

I mean nothing to them
my frenetic comings and goings
do not disturb
they are in it for the long haul
do not know that just gazing
on their might gives me
stability
hope
peace

## Santa Fe

Wispy clouds float by
under blue bowl of sky,
turquoise adornments on display
mirror its foreverness,
silver, sunshine dancing on green leaves.

Paintings in galleries show
rusty hills, adobe homes,
fuschia flowers, native spirit,
peace, alongside
poverty and despair.

Art once reflected life
but now throngs of shoppers and
foodies change the landscape
from insightful celebration
to greed and getting.

They come not to be in this place
but to take a bit of the magic
away.

## Mass. Ave.

I stroll your narrow sidewalks,
trip on lumpy black macadam
like a child again.
Imposing colonial homes
salt box, gables, clapboard lines
look smart and noble despite their age
but smell of mold and too many cats.
Neatly lettered signs tell
their provenance.
I respect longevity,
admire trees a hundred years old,
inhale serenity
of quiet, unassuming wealth.
I lose myself to the past.
White dogwoods, maple whirligigs,
lush gardens modestly pruned
pay homage to a need for order,
to simpler times.
Aged fieldstone walls
line the road,
whisper stories
of marching Redcoats,
resistant revolutionaries,
carriage wheels,

until engine sounds
and auto exhaust
bring me back
to now.

## Way Down South

take a desert
animals with built-in baby seats
spiny plants
chortling birds
coiled snakes
grubs in tree roots
swirling flies
all dying for a drop
praying for rain
bridges over
riverbeds of sand

put the desert
in the middle of the ocean
far from other species
far from stories left behind
far from escape
adventure
banishment

steal the land
from the natives
make them quaint
make them other
give them money

ignore their
souls, immersed in the land

put a smile on it
tell a joke about it
accept the power
of what you can't control

and you have
Australia

## Nicaragua Noise

the noise of dirt
intrudes:
dirt and squalor
hunger and want
stink of trash
walking through mud
flies on my food
discomfort
keeps me from being present
keeps me from hearing
what is in your beautiful eyes

Here in the countryside
with scorpions, skinny cows
starry nights
my compassion
cannot survive—
I need to escape
to clean and quiet
there is no space
for anything else.

# Sounds of the Valley

Whoosh of a hot air balloon overhead
Whistle of Wine Train
Twittering birds in the trees
Crunch of leaves underfoot
Roar of fans in early morning darkness
Rattle of trucks bearing wine down Hwy 29
Dogs barking on country roads
Drumming of rain on the deck
Rushing water in creeks
River lapping at oars
Tinkle of crystal
Clatter of dinnerware
Bistros, banquets,
Charity events
Cheering stadium crowds
Runners' feet slapping pavement
Wine glasses clinking a toast
Empty bottles crashing into bins
Bands and engines at every parade
Symphonies and string quartets
Arias bursting forth and jazz and
Children's choirs
And bedside song
Finally at midnight
Under a starlit dome
Silence that says
You can have it all

## Cobblestones

they blanket the streets
of ancient byways
like a carefully crafted quilt
uniform squares
rounded tops
gotta love 'em

no ruts
no mud
walkers hear
the wagon coming
hear the clip clop
of horse hooves
hear the heavy tires
of trucks

cobblestones
gotta love 'em
until you have to
walk on 'em
for hours
forget about high heels
even in tennies
they're a bitch

gimme asphalt
concrete, macadam
any old surface will do
just let my heel
and toe embrace
something flat

III.

# Tribes

Tribes stake claim
Claim human hearts
Bloods and Crips
Muslims and Jews
Marrieds and singles
Meat eaters and vegans
Tree huggers and oilmen
Gays and straights
Liberals and Neocons
Sissies and wife beaters—
All place blame

Do you hate...
Soldiers?
Drag queens?
Socialists?
CEOs?
Protestors?
Talk show hosts?
Latte drinkers?
Fundamentalists?

Whose hut feels like home?

Or perhaps one day we will
Open our eyes and hearts
Pass the peace pipe
Become one tribe
Brothers and sisters
Owning what we share:
      blood
      life
      destiny

## Indivisible

I am your brother
more than ever
it seems like yesterday
our days of tadpoles and lightning bugs
you following me to the fishing pond
following me to school
though I told you to
stay home

I am your brother
you follow me no more
I told you I was with the Union
cannot accept slavery
or the division of our great country

I am your brother
long gone when you joined the Rebs
just because your friends were going
to escape the boring farm
for an adventure

I am your brother
I looked over the field
for you today
after the battle, over the wounded
I wonder where you are

I do my best to beat your side
you to beat mine
we will each do our duty
I pray to see you again one day
you aren't my enemy

I am your brother

## Dear Hillary

How is your day?
I can't imagine any other way
than grim with agony and loss,
as you watch what has happened.
I, who only made phone calls
for three months
using crappy voter lists
from the DNC—don't get me started—
I'm so depressed, still.
Are you?
You did everything right:
right words—well, except *deplorables*—
right attitude, right smarts.
How is it possible to do everything right
and still lose?
Mom always said if I worked hard and was nice and did things right,
life would go my way.
It sort of has, although
I missed my chance to have kids
while dating a guy who already had
several and didn't want more.
If I could go back, I'd skip the
birth control and just get pregnant anyway.
I could have had a kid
who'd be forty years old now.
Heck, I'd be a grandma.

So, Hillary, do you just wake up every day
and say, "I didn't get what I wanted but I'm still worthy?"
Do you grouse about who cheated you out of it?
About the stupid electoral college?
Or are you just busy being a loving grandma,
taking a break from the craziness.
See, grandmas always have
something
meaningful
to
do.

## Election Day

hot dust rises like ocean fog
gravel crunching under tires
we peer into the morning, seek an address
reluctant couriers of change
sturdy house? ramshackle cabin?
one by one, we check our list,
disembark, listen for growling,
knock once and again
purposeful with doubt and fear
no one home, relief and disappointment blend.

gravel and dust meet golden aspen sky
aged trailers on cinder blocks
rusty equipment, goats in the yard
"Hi, sir, volunteers here. Sorry to bother you."
paper-covered windows hide something
fly-covered wall implies the worst
"Have you voted? Can we count on you?"
mud rooms filled with trash—
"Thanks for your support."

hot dust rises again as we depart
heart's heaviness gives way.
peace replaces helplessness
hope breaks free to float
above the hard-scrabble earth

IV.

# Sweat

no hugs at the gym, please
no cheek kisses, pats on the back—
mingling sweat is only
for the most intimate of
couplings
or Bay to Breakers
when it's the only way
to slide past another
runner in the throng
arm to arm
swapping sweat
lacking disgust
only because it feels
so good
(heart pounding in chest
legs pounding pavement)
to be
alive

## Self Storage

How do I store myself?
Let me count the ways:

one hundred bits of life
pasted into scrapbooks:
ticket stubs
railway passes
pressed flowers from a dance

forty Facebook photos
posted for the world to see
likes and smiley faces
telling friends
all is well
look at me

five bitter emotions
packed into scars you can't see
they hide
in social shyness
hesitance to reach out
fear of rejection

one solid determination
held deep in my soul
pushing me to
be true to my beliefs
ignore the crowd
speak against injustice

millions of words
words on paper, blogs
poems and stories
words that reveal all
or nothing
sweet and savory
kind and cruel
words that tell
anyone who will read them
who will try to understand
who I am

## Out of the Dark (room)

changing yourself is no hobby
not natural like a chameleon shedding its skin
or trees that sprout in spring

you look within
in the light
you can see the need
you can feel in your body
what it would be like to be different
to be kinder, softer, smarter

but unlike what you do with film
in the dark
expose the paper to the image
pour developer in the tray
and like magic
watch a picture appear
(perhaps even the picture you
had in your mind's eye)

your developer isn't
available on a shelf
but comes from deep within
you observe yourself
through the lens of determination

ask how did I do today
note your progress
(and hope the picture revealed
is just what you had in mind)

## The Right Crowd

fear of the closed off space
no exit
racing to the elevator at precisely
5 o'clock
to get to the street, the subway
away from the crowd
the mingle of humanity
going every which way
each with his own fiery intent
need to be first
pushing me out of the way
while I push others

no true claustrophobic
give me Bay to Breakers
a hundred thousand sweaty runners
exchanging arm juice as they slip past
running walking talking jostling
of one mind moving
in the same direction
endorphins fill the misty air
legs pump happiness

or put me at Spirit Rock
blessed presence of Thich Nhat Hanh
thousands on the grass before him
rise up in silence
follow his lead, turn
to walk
slow    as    a    snail
behind him
a drop of water in this wave of humanity
I am at peace, content
in love with the crowd

## Marianne's Earrings

a cache of memories
grandpa's harmonica
grandma's kitchen
smells and sounds and tastes

*What do* **I** *recall?*

strands of magic
a child remembers
woven together
and grounded
in small metal hoops

*What binds* **me** *to the past?*

remind her every day
of family
love
the Croatia
she never saw

*Where did* **I** *come from?*

earrings worn
by all the women
and girls
in the town
their town

*What place owns* **me**?

Marianne's town
never seen but felt
always
in her heart
earrings of
her soul

*Who will remember* **me**?

## Heart Geography

your tears
bring my tears
instantly
bleeding wounds
broken limbs
before my eyes
bring me
anguish
my heart calls out
for action
right now

yet show me photos
of people far away
crying
needing help
and I close my eyes
turn the page
shut it out

is it because I am
too far away
to put my arm around them?
too far away

to smell the sickness?
is it because they
can't rest their sorrowful eyes
on mine?

## Pianist

in the silent auditorium
a thousand pairs of ears and eyes
cleave the darkness
fix on you

red dress hugs your slender torso
ruffles cascading down your lap
belie the power rising
from your back
through spare strong arms
as fingers
assault the keys
lifting your body off the seat

You grab me propel me
into the music
crashing onto the keyboard
leaning back in fullness
into the surging pulling
swirling eddy of quicksand
into the music

we are the music
violins and oboes
background to our birthing
chords so profound
they suck tears from my eyes

and like the day a tunnel
spit me out onto a road
under full canopy
crimson sky
it is enough
from life
to know such joy

## In the Shadows

in my grandma years
I'm happy to sit in the shade
no bright sun for me
no spotlight, heat, no glare

in the shade
I comfortably watch
the play of sun in the trees
brilliant greens against the blues
hear the delicate rhythm
of the brook going by
watch aspen leaves like coins
dancing in a luscious breeze

in the shadows
I watch the young at play
running, teasing, giggling
growing up so fast
they don't notice me
don't hear my questions
don't need my approval
they have their own voice

I contemplate my place
not in a game or race or struggle
but in the greater meaning of
living for almost seventy years
being part of nature's scheme
coming into the world
growing, striving, doing
then resting, withering, dying

I am happy to sit in the shade
to feel, to see, to be me

V.

## Leaning on Me

I stand at the sink
you walk behind
not to embrace
not to whisper
"I love you"
like long ago
so quietly
I almost didn't hear
but simply
to rest your head
your weary head
on my shoulder
so full of worry
fear and pain
as if you would
transfer some
to me
and
although I feel the
intimacy
the touch
the connection
more than anything
I feel the weight

## Negation

don't "no" me
don't turn your head
close your ears
walk away from
who I am and
what I say
lost in your own mind
not knowing anything
but you

don't form your
own thoughts
while I look into
your eyes and struggle
to get out my words
my precious words
that mean so much to me
if only you could
open up enough to hear

if you listen, will you know me?
I may wonder always
but please don't "no" me.

# In the Mirror

*When I look in the mirror, who is there?*

Mom quit school early
helped at home
worked in a store
took a class, got some skills
found a better job
met Dad, the wise guy
hated him, loved him, married him
had me a year later
then my brother

*She looks back at me, smiling*

finished high school by
mail order
studied drawing and painting
quit smoking but
squirreled away the money
she might have spent for years
increased it when the
price went up
bought me a car with that money
when I was twenty

*I look back at that beloved face, now my own*

grunted to Jack LaLanne on the floor
in front of the TV to flatten her tummy
and twisted her face into horrors
to avoid neck wrinkles
learned to drive at sixty
used coupons, opened bank accounts

*I know where I come from*

bought her own lap pool
that Dad didn't want
and the blue rug no
decorator would recommend
rode a big trike to fight
her diabetes
collected cans for money
supported African orphans

*I'm still her student*

she only wanted to
      look better
           learn
                do good things

*I see her in the mirror and say*
*Yes!*

## To My Brother

one birthday
a boy and a girl
two years apart
one party, two cakes
matching cowboy suits
two dolls, two toy horses
love and attention
in equal parts

name calling
knocking each other to the ground
teasing and yelling
tearing each other down
wearing our jealousies deep
unlike our jaunty cowboy hats

I'd rather remember
giggles
tickles
friendship
solidarity against
adult control

two guitars
east coast west coast
strumming different songs
weaving joy and pain
grieving lost connections
separate lives
a man and a woman
one birthday

## Grandma

she lay on the bed
hunched back, mended hip
confined yet sparkling
like a well tuned music box
humming to radio opera I didn't understand
Cavelleria Rusticana
Gilbert and Sullivan
Strauss waltzes

a small child
no ballerina
I danced around the living room
to those tunes
they gladden my heart today
she sang from her own youth
"The Melancholy Marshmallow"
songs she could no longer play on the piano
from sheet music I've played
then framed to hang on the wall
telling stories of her flirtations
asking about my boyfriends
wanting romance for me too

she complained
not of her pain

except the "oy oy" when she had to
rise from the bed
but about the maids
who didn't last
because they helped themselves
to silver, jewelry, precious things
about her rich sister
who married well
several times, lived in the
same building as
Harry Belafonte
or about food someone prepared
a whole beef tongue
resting lifelike on its plate
capturing my eyes
turning my stomach

she set the standard for all
mistress of her table
one day I said, "I'm stuffed."
"You are not stuffed,"
she reprimanded,
"You've had sufficient."

## After You Spent the Night

*Your soft breath on my shoulder*
> I dress with care for your party
> smile at myself in the mirror
> snug jeans, slight cleavage
> burning with new love

*Morning light erased the darkness*
> you greet me at the door and are gone
> rooms full of women
> I wait for your attention
> slowly realize it won't come

*One last caress*
> one more conquest
> notch on your bedpost
> how could I be so dumb
> dash for the door

*And you were gone*
> alone at home my anger
> cracks me open
> so foolish to believe our time together
> meant something
> to you

## One-Dog Night

Warm bodies,
snuggle buddies
relax together
hear heartbeats,
wrapped in limbs,
embrace warmth,
comfort in each other.

We drift back
to mother's embrace,
perhaps the womb—
place of comfort and promise,
perception of life,
although we know nothing,
so strong, so sure
protected and safe,
loved and nourished.

Explains why we like bear hugs,
shoulders to lean on,
caressing hands.
So lie still, little buddy
and let me hold you,
while knowing deep down
you are holding me.

## Wedding Party

I.  a snow-petal vision in white
    floats down the aisle on Dad's arm
    like her first communion
    all sparkly eyes and open heart
    but some of us know the true
    shape of this bride's soul

II.  she should have picked the other dress
    more flattering to her shape
    she wants to look sexy on this day?
    the strapless tease, low back, dark eyes
    no flowers in her hair
    I knew him first
    could have been me up there

III.  as a baby all peaches and cream
    sunny smile, wispy blond fluff, pink
        cheeks
    smelled like fresh pastry
    today it's all for the cameras:
    style, make-up, sprayed hair
    where is the darling child who asked
    Can I be a princess too?

IV.      her upper lip quivers
just a hint of nerves
soon the performance will end
and we can go back to the everyday
that we do so well
just the two of us, leaning on each other
she'll be mine
as long as I can hold her attention

V.      one more step
then the ring and the vows
one more step
the bird fluttering in my chest will sing
no more just me alone
no excuses to be made
shame to be delayed
just the two of us
one more step
to the rest
of my life

## Principal's Toes

This queen of the castle
from my childhood
sits on my treatment chair,
once powerful grey head
bowed over her task,
removes shoes and socks,
no sultry strip tease,
just a simple request
with sorrow, bare feet
what can I do?

those feet knew so much
walked hallways and school grounds
patrolled bleachers and bathrooms
mile upon mile upon mile
dressed in heels, pumps
sandals, tennis shoes

kicked balls
stood for assemblies
surveyed softball
visited the class
to tell us important things
about learning
and men with guns

she retired but
her feet and toes
continued their travels
flew over oceans
walked cobblestones
from Paris to Pretoria
discovered the world

those toes
now bent and red
look tired and sore
they've done their bit
like weary soldiers
ready for R & R

I hope she doesn't see
my face flush as I
lay on my hands for
solace, release from pain
and thanks

## Cravings at Seventy

I. I want to lean on you
if I'm not too heavy
like a cupboard leans on a wall
everything inside me
needing a promise of support
I want to ask you to dwarf my pain
make me feel safe
smother my fears
in your warm blanket
just for a moment
as if I were still a treasured child
asleep in the car and carried
to my bed
I want you to be the one who can make
everything OK

II. too old to be carried, asleep
to my bed
too alone to ask for a shoulder
to lean into
yet still I seek comfort
in song
from violins
or novels

or the presence of
strangers
I may look brave
and strong
but I am still that
child
wanting to be wrapped
in mother's embrace
and told it will all be OK

VI.

## Big or Small

my mind is as big
as the universe, expanding
to take it all in—
classmates seated around me
Jim tapping his foot
A/C throbbing in the background
parking lot full of cars
red and brown and grey
students wearing shorts
strolling in May heat
city alive with workers
kids getting out of school
visitors savoring wine
blood-red and full-bodied

to the breadth of a nation
farmers working squares
of green and gold
businessmen on phones
in columns of steel
where twilight falls
across the planet
millions sleeping

dream of yesterdays
or wake to smell their morning coffee

to the cold darkness
of the solar system
without wind or life
seen by reflected light
of stars incredibly
far away, where my mind is
a meaningless blip
of energy—
it arrived in an instant
will leave the same way

## Gates and Chimneys

It's a tragedy when people are wiped out
killed in an accident far from home
knocked down by crime or illness
leaving behind a life's collection of
things

Heirs sift through stuff
furniture, papers, clothing
smell years of mildewed milestones
decide what to keep and what to
lose

It's different when the stuff is gone
taken by fire, and people who survive have
only gates and chimneys
from a lifetime of
memories

Victims stand in charred emptiness
remember furniture, papers, clothing
smelling only soot and ash
wonder how to get beyond the
loss

## My Journey with Grief

I have traveled far with grief
I have wrapped my arms around
my still-warm love
denying his last breath
I have held my mother's hands,
hands that held mine so many times
still soft, but cool, ribbed with veins
and felt her fall away
I have said, "I love you, Dad"
so rarely, but special this time
for soon he too was gone
I have sat at friend's bedside
on her last day and gave a gift:
"Don't try to open your eyes"
over and over and over
I have seen everything
becoming nothing
unable to provide relief
my life continues on in grief

## Reprise

old dog's sweetness
makes my heart swell
ten years of love spilling over
because you're going soon

I hold
each warm moment
each caress of soft fur
each lick of your gentle tongue
in cupped hands like a desert wanderer
savoring my last precious drops of water

adoring eyes melt into
adoring eyes and
just like with the man
who went before
every blissful sip
contains a drop
of pain

# I Summoned Death

I summoned Death
made an appointment
planned ahead
from the depths of my
sorrow, knowing it
was time to
let him go, made
a pact with nevermore
not knowing how often
I would regret it
want to regress
postpone
have just a few more hours
filled with pain
his and mine
never truly ready
for what Death
leaves behind

## Leavings

new ballet slippers, size 4
wrapped in soft paper
pink ribbons hidden in a box
in the hall closet
waiting for her next birthday

theater tickets purchased
long ago, great expense
small envelope in desk drawer
a play he longed to see
promising a night to remember

book half read on the nightstand
page turned down
just before the climax
smoldering
for completion

dirty laundry
nobody should touch
in the back of the closet
stinking of sweaty socks
basketball, the track

secret letters, unpaid bills
evidence of sloth, deceit
wanting privacy, not meant
for others' eyes
even loved ones

heirs and survivors
left with it all
to sort and toss
between their tears
"I didn't know"

...because we always think we're coming back

## Five

If tragedy doesn't strike,
the first five years
are a miracle of evolution
eyes and ears open to
the feast of sensations in our world
we learn about other people, places
animals, food, music
we become creatures who walk
beings who talk, to say
what we want
find joy in games and stories and toys
we prosper when someone holds us
or sings to us with affection

If tragedy doesn't strike,
the last five years
are a sorrow pit of decay
we cannot trust our eyes and ears
to give us what we need
we forget what we have known
lose interest in the world
can't get anyone's attention
have difficulty walking
can't find words
want more company

or only to be left alone
find joy in moments free from pain
or when someone holds us
or sings to us with affection

## Death in Three Acts, in No Particular Order

III.
the awkward feeling
out of sorts, something missing
his presence anticipated
but no longer here
throughout each day
little reminders of
how it used to be, the pain of
how it is now
less, lonely, lost


I.
watching him struggle
day by day
the beauty of life's effort
to keep going
the sadness: knowing what
is coming, sooner or later
wondering what it will be like
planning for it
cherishing each moment
together
deep happiness holding tears

II.
the moment of death
anticipated for so long
but still a surprise
shock to find suddenly
the spark is extinguished
leaving only a corpse
the one I loved so deeply
is gone
the image of the moment
burned into my memory
forever

## Keepsake

the ring
burning bright in my hand
plain single band
yellow gold, engraved
old, more than fifty years
one more year than I

the ring compels me to speak
near dawn
standing at the foot of
Dad's bed
in the nursing home
waiting for his eyes to open
in this sad room

the ring, removed
a few hours before
from Mom's finger
after hurried flight
across the country
heart pressed
to arrive at the hospital
in time

the ring, small and fragile
useless
without her
needing to be returned
to its partner
not to be lost when
they take her body
away

the ring, turning it over
and over
in my impatient hand
loathe to speak
too hard
to bear this news

his eyes open
he sees me
without words, understands
lets out one sharp yelp
then silence
I hold out my
offering of love

## Absence

missing you is

my fingertips
remembering
your warmth

wisps of your hair
on my pillow
your scent in the air

my ears listening
for footsteps
that aren't there

expecting a greeting
when I arrive home
to find none

your shirt on the door
shoes on the floor
cup in the sink

no eyes to look
into mine
and know

everything

## Prayer for Dying

this massive darkness
beckons me, welcomes me
and I welcome it

every day, let me see the light from the window
shining into my room
throwing shadow and shapes on the floor

but at night, don't cover the window
let me eat the darkness
let it seep into the room
let it melt into my open arms
and make me one with eternal rest

## Joints

not the roast on the
Sunday dinner table
after church

not the place
where you go
to hang out
listen to some jazz
throw back a few

not the kind you
get sent to
for doing something
against the law
even if you didn't do it

not the kind you smoke
in some private place
with your best bud
so you can get into the
music or the conversation
and giggle 'til you
pee your pants
then eat a pizza

not even the beautiful juncture
of two pieces of wood in your favorite
chair

but the kind that connect
your arms and legs
so they can bend and move
and carry you where
you need to go
so you can get up from the chair
after the meal or the music
swing a punch for defense
when assaulted
dance your heart out
when you're high

if only you were a puppet
whose joints
could be fixed with
a little oil or
by loosening a screw

once yours are worn
there's just no telling
how long you can stand
or stand it

# *Leavings*

perhaps a few drinks
a few tokes
a few tunes
a good meal
or imagining whom
you'd like to punch
will ease your pain

## Steep

White blissful spires
poke through scenic green of
New England towns—
steep-les point to God.

Climbing the hill
so steep you wonder why
you started up
but know you'll be elated at the top.

"Too steep," she said,
glancing at the market goods,
shook her head,
waited for a bargain to be struck.

Steep the leaves just right—
too long and it's bitter,
too short and it's still
water.

## there's no parking in my heart

you are free to idle for a while
rev your engine, take a look around
take me for a ride

just don't unload anything too big or heavy
and while you're here
don't expect to upload anything
I have nothing to give away

you can wait, but keep it short
if you're not careful
you might run out of gas
or find you've overstayed
and you'll be towed away

there's no parking in my heart

# Gun Story

revolver, twenty-two caliber
resting on the table
clean and cold
quiet as earth's iron
ready to fire
bullets asleep in sturdy chambers
in this house of death
dream of possibility
imagine the explosion of blood
splintered bone
a corpse
with a story to tell

a story to tell
a corpse
splintered bone
explosion of blood
dreams of reality
in this house of death
bullets escaped sturdy chambers
already fired
quiet as earth's iron
clean and cold
resting on the table
twenty-two caliber revolver

# INDEX

# INDEX

# INDEX

## ABOUT THE AUTHOR

Lenore Hirsch had a successful career as a teacher and school administrator before retiring in 2005. Since then, she has written columns and features for the *Napa Valley Register*, blogs about her dogs and Napa Valley restaurants, and has published poetry, memoir, short stories, food and travel pieces. In 2013 she published *My Leash on Life, Foxy's View of the World from a Foot Off the Ground*. She is working on a collection of essays about the humor in aging. Contact her through www.lenorehirsch.com or lenorehirsch@att.net.